GW01425272

Paint & Paper
Crafts

Gloria McKinnon

Contents

Editorial
Managing Editor: Judy Poulos
Contributing Editor: Gloria McKinnon

Photography: Andrew Payne, Andrew Elton
Styling: Louise Owens, Kathy Tripp,
Lisa Hilton, Anne-Marie Unwin
Illustrations: Lesley Griffith

Production and Design
Production Director: Anna Maguire
Design Manager: Drew Buckmaster
Production Coordinator: Meredith Johnston
Production Artists: Petra Rode, Lulu Dougherty
Assistant Designer: Sheridan Packer
Junior Production Editor: Heather Straton

Published by J.B. Fairfax Press, an imprint of
LibertyOne Media Group Pty Limited
80-82 McLachlan Ave
Rushcutters Bay, Australia 2011
A.C.N. 078 084 447
Web Address: http://www.jbfp.com.au

Formatted by J.B. Fairfax Press
Printed by Toppan Printing Co. Hong Kong

© LibertyOne Media Group Pty Limited 1999

Enquiries should be made in writing to the
publisher. The information in this book is
provided in good faith with no guarantee implied

Some of the material in this book has been
previously published in other J.B. Fairfax Press
Pty Limited publications.
JBFP 537

PAINT & PAPER CRAFTS
ISBN 1 86343 366 X

DISTRIBUTION AND SALES
Australia: J.B. Fairfax Press
Ph: (02) 9361 6366; Fax: (02) 9360 6262
USA: Quilter's Resource Inc
2211 Nth Elston Ave, Chicago 60614
Ph: (773) 278 5695; Fax: (773) 278 1348

Paint & Paper Crafts

Applying paint to paper or a wooden surface is one of the oldest of the decorative arts. This book draws together a collection of delightful projects that use paint and paper.

Folk art has always been the mode of artistic expression for common folk and the designs usually reflect these origins. Folk art painting requires no great skill or learning as the design and the order of painting are provided. In fact, the 'mistakes' often add to the charm of the piece. The projects presented here range from a cute bear family, dressed in all their finery, to a delicate lace fan, ideal for framing.

Paper is a fabulous craft medium. It is inexpensive, readily available and comes in a wonderful variety of weights and textures. Composed of cut-out images which have been glued down, then varnished, découpage has long been used to decorate simple objects. Begin with a small piece, such as the spectacle case, then graduate to the mirror frame decorated with roses.

Wisteria Box

MADE BY PIECEMAKERS STORE, CALIFORNIA

This easy treatment with pretty stamps will create a wonderful box quickly.

Materials

- 38 cm (15 in) round wooden box with lid
- wisteria rubber decorator block set
- artist's flat brush
- artist's pointed round brush
- decorator glaze: Green, Lilac, Gold
- FolkArt Acrylic Colors, Wicker White for the base coat
- FolkArt Spray Acrylic Sealer, matte

Method

1 Paint the box with two coats of Wicker White, allowing the paint to dry thoroughly between each coat.

2 With the dry flat brush and the absolute bare minimum of Gold paint, brush lightly and randomly over the base coat to give an antique look. Allow to dry.

3 With the flat brush, apply Green paint quite liberally to the leaf rubber block, on the side with the veins.

For the lid

1 Stamp the leaves, creating two groups of seven or eight leaves. You should be able to stamp three or four leaves before you need to reload with paint. This way you will have shading in the leaves. Reload the paint and continue.

2 When the leaves are quite dry, stamp the flowers. Load the Lilac paint onto the flower block. Stamp one large flower head with approximately forty-eight small flowers, and the other smaller one with approximately twenty-eight flowers. The flowers should be shaped like a teardrop.

3 Stamp the leaves on the side of the lid so some of them come onto the lid top.

4 When all the flowers and leaves are dry, using the round brush, paint some Green tendrils and some Gold tendrils around the design.

Finishing

Complete the box sides in the same manner as the lid, making smaller flower and leaf arrangements. When all the paint is dry, spray the box with the sealer.

Stencilled Wallhanging

MADE BY COUNTRY STENCILS, USA

Simple stencilling, using tin stencils, makes this delightful country-style wallhanging. You can make your own stencils from the pattern on the pattern sheet or you can purchase the tin stencils.

Finished size: 32.5 cm x 38 cm (12³/₄ in x 15 in)

Materials

- 26.5 cm x 31.5 cm (10¹/₂ in x 12¹/₂ in) of background fabric, such as ticking
- four strips of fabric, each 2 cm x 50 cm (³/₄ in x 20 in), for the first border
- four strips of fabric, each 2.5 cm x 50 cm (1 in x 20 in), for the second border
- 39 cm x 44.5 cm (15¹/₄ in x 17¹/₂ in) of backing fabric
- 32.5 cm x 38 cm (12³/₄ in x 15 in) of Pellon
- 26.5 cm x 31.5 cm (10¹/₂ in x 12¹/₂ in) sheets of clear Mylar
- craft knife
- stencil brush
- acrylic paints in the colours of your choice or a multicoloured stamp pad
- Pigma pen, Black
- 30 cm (12 in) long leather thong
- tin Country Garden stencils
- stylus or toothpick
- small sew-on tin stencils (we used a rabbit and a 'Herb' sign)
- two small brass rings for hanging or a length of wooden dowel

Method

See the Pattern on the Pull Out Pattern Sheet.

1 Trace the window frame, table, drying rack, wall plaque, crock and large terracotta pot onto one sheet of Mylar. Cut them out carefully. Trace and cut out the pegs on the drying rack and the small terracotta pots on a separate sheet of Mylar.

2 Lay the first stencil onto the background fabric. Using only a very small amount of paint or ink on a dry stencil brush, stencil in the window frame, table, drying rack, wall plaque, crock and large terracotta pot. When that paint is dry, apply the second stencil and colour in the pegs and the small terracotta pots.

3 With an almost-dry stencil brush, smudge in the shape of the wreaths.

4 Using the tin stencils, stencil the basket first, then the leaves or the flowers. Paint in the details, using the end of a stylus or toothpick. (You can make Mylar stencils of these pieces as well, if you don't wish to use tin stencils.)

5 Using the Pigma pen, print 'Beyond the garden gate' on the wall plaque.

6 Stitch on the small sew-on stencils and a bow tied with the leather thong.

Finishing

1 Sew on the two borders, using 6 mm (¹/₄ in) seams, sewing on the side borders first, then the top and bottom borders.

2 Lay the backing face down with the Pellon on top and the completed front on top of that, face upwards. Note that the backing extends beyond the edges of the front piece. Fold the backing onto the front, turning in 6 mm (¹/₄ in) on the raw edges and mitring the corners as you go. Slipstitch this edge onto the front, stitching through the Pellon but not through the backing. Press the borders.

3 Hand-sew the rings to the back of the wallhanging or make a sleeve from fabric for the length of wooden dowel.

Bear Family Portrait

PAINTED BY ANNETTE MANSFIELD

This delightful design has been painted on a wooden writing case; you could paint the same picture on any rectangular surface. The design is reminiscent of the holiday portraits, popular early this century, where family members peeped through the cut-outs in a painted scene – except this time, we have a family of bears!

Materials

- ❦ a suitable box
- ❦ transfer paper
- ❦ fineline permanent marker pen
- ❦ stylus
- ❦ pencil
- ❦ sandpaper, fine
- ❦ FolkArt Colors: Taffy, Apple Spice
- ❦ Jo Sonja's Artists Colors: Raw Sienna, Burnt Sienna, Burgundy, Prussian Blue, Black, Titanium White, Gold Oxide, Teal Green, Indian Red Oxide
- ❦ antiquing medium
- ❦ oil paint, Burnt Umber
- ❦ cotton rags
- ❦ Harvest Tole matte spray varnish
- ❦ round brush, size 2
- ❦ liner brushes, sizes 1, 00, 10/0
- ❦ slant shader brush, size 3
- ❦ deerfoot brush, 6 mm (1/4 in)
- ❦ sponge brush
- ❦ tack cloth
- ❦ Clag paste
- ❦ PVA adhesive

Method

See the Painting Design on the Pull Out Pattern Sheet and the Work Sheets on pages 10 – 16.

Preparation

1 Using the sponge brush, base coat the outside of the box with two coats of Taffy. Using the same brush, base coat the inside of the box with two coats of Apple Spice.

2 Trace the design from the pattern sheet and transfer it to the lid of the box, using the transfer paper and stylus.

Base coating

Following work sheet 1 and using the round brush, paint in the bears' clothing as follows. You will need to apply two or three coats to ensure a good coverage. Leave a very narrow gap between areas of the same colour to define the parts – for example, on the mother bear's arm and dress.

Note: When painting any part of the bears or their clothing, apply the paint in the appropriate direction; for example, paint down the length of a skirt, not across, and paint around the muzzles, not up and down.

1 *Mother bear* The dress is Burgundy and the scarf is Black. The hat is Prussian Blue with a touch of Titanium White.

2 *Father bear* The coat is Prussian Blue mixed with a touch of Titanium White. The vest is a 3:1 mixture of Prussian Blue and Titanium White. The coat collar is Prussian Blue mixed with a touch of Black. The pants and the hat are Titanium White mixed with a touch of Raw Sienna. Paint the handle of the cane Black. Do not paint the collar or the cravat at this stage.

3 *Little girl bear* The dress and collar are Titanium White mixed with Burgundy to create a strong pink. The bodice is Titanium White. The cuff is a lighter version of the colour of the dress. The hat is Raw Sienna.

4 Base coat the faces and paws in Raw Sienna.

Shading the clothing

Following work sheet 2 and using the slant shader brush, float in the highlights and shadows as follows. These floats should fill in the small gaps left in the base coats.

1 *Mother bear* Float a medium pink mixture of Burgundy and Titanium White down the inside of the arm, and down the edge of the bodice to define the chest. Float some

folds in the skirt in the same colour. Using the round brush, add a light patch to the edge of the paw with a mixture of Titanium White and Raw Sienna. Using the round brush, paint a Black wash on the underside of the hat. (You will see this more clearly on work sheet 3.)

2 **Father bear** Paint a light blue float with a mix of Prussian Blue and Titanium White down the right side of both sleeves and around the outer edge of the collar. Paint in some soft creases down the left side of the trouser leg and under the knee with a mix of Raw Sienna and Titanium

White. Paint a very thin line of Black down the inside of the arm holding the cane. Paint small Black dots for the vest buttons, using the end of the handle of a paintbrush. With a liner brush, paint a line down the centre of the vest with thin Black paint. With the round brush, paint a wash of Raw Sienna on the underside of the hat and on the right-hand side of the hat. Following work sheet 4, using the round brush and Prussian Blue side-loaded with Titanium White, paint in the folds of the cravat. Paint the collar in Titanium White, outlined in Black.

Work sheet 1

3 *Little girl bear* Float deep pink shadows in a mix of Burgundy and Titanium White down both sides of the sleeve, making a fold effect at the elbow. Float the same colour on the collar just under the chin. Float deep pink shadows across the waist of the dress and on some folds in the skirt. Using the end of the paintbrush handle, place some thick Titanium White dots on the bodice and let these dry before proceeding to the next step. With very thin Black paint, float over some of the shadows to give them more depth. Float a shadow on the arm side of the bodice and under the collar.

Using the size 00 liner brush and Black, outline the cuff. Using the size 1 liner brush and thin light pink (Titanium White and a touch of Burgundy) paint in the hoop. Using the round brush, paint a wash of Gold Oxide on the underside of the hat.

Painting paws and faces

1 Following work sheet 2 and using the size 00 liner brush and thin Black paint, paint in the claws. With a thin mix of Titanium White and Raw Sienna, and a liner brush, paint very fine hairs around the outside of the paws.

Work sheet 3

2 Following work sheets 3, 4 and 5 and using the slant shader brush, float Burnt Sienna down the left side of each face and around each muzzle. Float the same colour across under each hat. For a highlight, float a light mix of Titanium White and Raw Sienna down the right side of each face.

3 Paint the fur with the size 10/0 liner brush and thin paint. Beginning on the left side of each face and using a mix of Burnt Sienna and Black, paint in the fur with a criss-cross motion. Try not to make these strokes too tidy, but keep them fine. Work three or four rows, working towards the centre of the face with this mix, then change to Burnt Sienna and continue across the middle of the face. At first, the Burnt Sienna rows should overlap the previous coloured rows to give a graduated colour change.

4 Using the same technique, paint in the fur on the right side of the face with a mix of Titanium White with a touch of Raw Sienna. Note that this time you are beginning with a light colour at the edge and moving towards the darker colour (Burnt Sienna) as you approach the middle of the face.

5 When all the fur detail is painted on the faces, detail the muzzles in the same way. The first dark brown row should extend over the face slightly.

6 Using the round brush, paint the eyes and noses in Black then, using the size 00 liner brush and Black, paint the mouths. Following work sheet 5, highlight the eyes with Titanium White. Using a small brush and thin Titanium White, add the shine to each nose.

Painting the hats

1 *Mother bear* Following work sheet 3 and using the slant shader brush, float a highlight of Titanium White and Prussian Blue along the brim and the crown. Using the round brush, paint the hat band in a mix of Burgundy and Titanium White.

2 *Father bear* Following work sheet 4 and using the slant shader, float a shadow down the right side of the hat in a mix of Raw Sienna with a touch of Titanium White. Float a highlight down the other side of the hat with Titanium White. Using the round brush and a watery mix of Raw Sienna and Titanium White, deepen the ends of the brim to define the shape. Paint the hat band Prussian Blue.

3 *Little girl bear* Following work sheet 5 and using the slant shader brush, float a shadow of Burnt Sienna down the left side of the crown. Highlight the right side with a thin float of Titanium White. Float Black shadows under the brim. With the size 00 liner brush and a thin mix of Burnt Sienna and Black, paint in the wavy lines and outline the brim. Paint the ribbons and the bow in a mix of Titanium White and Burgundy.

For the details

1 *Feather and scarf* Following work sheet 6 and using the round brush, base coat the feather with a wash of Prussian Blue. Take care to stay well within the tracing lines. When the base coat is dry, use the size 00 liner brush to pull long thin lines from the centre vein. Keep building the feather in this way until it becomes quite thick and full with the centre darker than the edges. With the end of the handle of a

Work sheet 4

Work sheet 5

paintbrush, paint Burgundy dots down both sides of the scarf to the point. Using the size 00 liner brush and thin Black, paint in the fringe on the scarf. Using the handle again, paint in two rows of thick Black dots, one row close to the fringe and the other row inside the row of Burgundy dots. If the dots flatten out as they dry, paint them again so that they stand out. Using the round brush, paint a small Titanium White oval for the base of the brooch. Surround the base with thick Titanium White dots painted in the same way as the other dots. With a liner brush, add a squiggle of Black to the centre of the brooch.

2 *Ink pot and quill* Following work sheet 7, paint the quill in the same way as the feather, using Gold Oxide. Fill in the tip of the quill with Gold Oxide on the round brush. Paint the outline of the ink pot with a thin wash of Teal Green. When this wash is dry, go over it again on the left side, the ink and the top of the pot to darken them. Outline the ink pot with Teal Green, using the size 00 liner brush.

3 *Scrolls and heart* Following work sheet 7 and using the size 1 liner brush and Gold Oxide, outline the heart and paint in the scrolls. To paint the scrolls, begin at the tip of the

14

curl and work back towards the other end. Using the handle of the paintbrush, put a dot of Gold Oxide at the end of each curl.

For the box

1 *Sides of the box* Transfer the checked design from the pattern sheet to both sides of the box. Following work sheet 7, paint alternate squares in thin Teal Green; you may need two coats. Allow the paint to dry, then sand the sides only in a top-to-bottom direction until you can see a little of the Taffy base coat showing through. Using the round brush, paint the hearts in Indian Red Oxide.

2 *Front, drawer and top* Paint a thin coat of Teal Green over the Taffy base coat. When this is dry, sand lightly until a little of the Taffy base coat shows through. Sand only in one direction – across the box. Wipe off any sanding residue. Using the round brush, paint the heart in Indian Red Oxide and outline it in Teal Green. Paint the drawer knob, the bottom edge of the box, the edges of the lid and the drawer in Indian Red Oxide.

3 *Inside lid* Transfer the design from the pattern sheet, taking care to ensure that it will be the right way up when the lid is opened. Find a suitable teddy bear card or picture and cut it to fit the oval frame. Transfer the message to a piece of art paper or parchment paper. Trace over the lines with a pencil, then cut it out. Glue the message in place with a 2:1 mix of Clag and PVA adhesive. Wipe off any excess glue. Glue the 'photo' inside the frame. Following work sheet 8, paint the frame in Gold Oxide, using the size 1 liner brush. Paint the wooden end of the pencil in a mix of Gold Oxide and Titanium White. When this is dry, paint in the lead with Black. With the size 1 liner brush, paint two dark green and two light green stripes, using varying mixes of Teal Green and Titanium White. Paint the end of the pencil in Black. Using the deerfoot brush and Raw Sienna, pounce in the paw prints. Go over them with Gold Oxide to add depth.

Finishing

1 When all the paint is dry, erase any visible transfer lines. Wipe the box all over with the tack cloth, then apply two light coats of the matte varnish, inside and out.

2 Antique the box with the antiquing medium and the oil paint. When the antiquing is dry, spray the box with a final coat of varnish.

Work sheet 6

Work sheet 7

Work sheet 8

Box with Roses

PAINTED BY ANNETTE JOHNSON

Embellish even the simplest box with these wonderful roses for an elegant transformation.

Materials

- Deco Art paints, Uniform Blue
- Jo Sonja's Artists Colors: Smoked Pearl, Napthol Crimson, Burnt Umber, Titanium White, Cod Yellow Medium, Ultra Blue Deep, Carbon Black, Yellow Oxide
- Easycraft Satin Varnish
- Weathered Wood Crackle Medium
- sea sponge
- flat brush, size 2.5 cm (1 in)
- flat brush, size 6
- round brush, size 2
- liner brush
- wet and dry sandpaper
- blue saral paper
- stylus
- wooden box

Method

See the Painting Design on page 21.

Preparation

1 Base coat the box with two coats of Uniform Blue, using the large flat brush. Sand lightly between coats.

2 Apply crackle medium randomly all over the box and let it dry.

Painting

1 Sponge Smoked Pearl over the entire box with a damp sponge. Let it dry thoroughly before transferring the pattern onto the box with the blue saral paper and the stylus.

2 Stipple some dark green paint (a mix of Ultra Blue, Black and Cod Yellow) beneath the leaf area, using the round brush. The leaves are painted with this same mix – vary the colour by adding more Titanium White or Cod Yellow. All overstrokes on the large leaves are painted with the round brush. Load the brush with the dark green paint mix and side-load with various mixes of Cod Yellow and Titanium White; add some Napthol Crimson and Burnt Umber for added interest.

3 Base coat the roses with a mix of Burnt Umber and Napthol Crimson.

4 Paint all the pink roses with the flat brush. Load half the brush with Napthol Crimson and Burnt Umber and the other half with Titanium White. Blend the colours well before painting. Paint the white rose with Burnt Umber and Titanium White. Tint with the pink rose colour when it's dry.

5 Paint the centres of the roses with small dots of Yellow Oxide and Titanium White.

6 Paint the top edge of the box lid with a wash of Uniform Blue. Using the flat brush, float Burnt Umber around all the edges. When the paint is dry, varnish the box.

A.A. Johnson ©96

Painting Design

Victorian Mirror

MADE BY KATH CONNELL

Elegant and romantic, this mirror would make a lovely focal point.

Materials

- raw wood frame and mirror
- flat brush, 2.5 cm (1 in) wide
- sponge
- fine sandpaper
- Jo Sonja's Artist's Colors: Blush (base coat), Storm Blue, Pine Green, Rich Gold
- palette (a tile or saucer will do)
- Clag paste
- PVA adhesive
- plastic container (an ice-cream container is ideal)
- kitchen cloth, such as Chux
- disposable plastic cup
- several ice-block sticks
- one small Envirotex
- Liquitex Gloss or Satin Varnish
- plastic sheet
- Victorian Rose paper
- spray-on sealer
- small sharp scissors
- rubber roller
- sharp blade
- brushes for varnish and for glue

Method

1 Remove the mirror from the frame and put it aside for safekeeping.

2 Base coat the frame (front and back) in Blush. If your frame has narrow ridges or grooves, like this one has, take care that the paint does not fill them up.

3 Place a small amount of Storm Blue and Pine Green on your palette. Using the clean brush, wet the edges of the frame. Side-load the brush with a little Storm Blue, stroking it on the palette until the colour is blended, then, while the frame is still damp, lightly stroke the edges, keeping the colour to the outside. Allow to dry. Repeat the process, using Pine Green around the inner edges. Allow to dry. You can also sponge a little colour on the centre of the frame, but remember to be very sparing and keep the sponge very damp. Allow to dry.

4 Seal the paper with the spray-on sealer. Cut out the roses, cutting with the curve of the scissors away from you to give a clean cut with no visible white edge. Cut single roses, clusters, leaves and stems.

5 Arrange the design on the frame, so that it is well-balanced and so that no particular rose 'jumps out' at you. Carefully lift off the roses and place them on a clean surface in the same arrangement. The last rose lifted off will be the first one glued down.

6 Fill the plastic container with water and place the cloth inside.

7 Mix equal quantities of Clag and PVA adhesive. Working on only a small area at a time and, using the paintbrush, apply a little of the glue mixture to the frame. Place the rose on the glue, then add a little more glue over the top. Using your thumb, gently rub from the centre of the rose to its edges, pushing out the excess glue. Wipe over the surface with the wet kitchen cloth to remove the excess glue. Run over the rose again lightly with the rubber roller, then wipe again with the cloth. Continue in this way until all the roses are in position, then glue on the stems and leaves to fill the gaps. Allow the glue to dry.

8 Apply two coats of varnish, drying between coats, to ensure that the Envirotex does not penetrate the paper.

9 Thoroughly clean up your work area and cover your work surface with the plastic sheet before the next step. Raise the frame up (on a book, cans, brick etc). Mix the Envirotex in the plastic container, using one of the ice-block sticks. Carefully pour the mixture down the centre of the frame, coaxing it to the edge (but not over it) with another clean stick. Then, take the mixture to the inner edge, allowing it to drip over. It will continue to drip for approximately ten to fifteen minutes, during which time you should continue to wipe off the drips with a clean stick. While the dripping continues, exhale gently over the frame. Tiny bubbles will rise to the surface. Continue exhaling over the frame until the surface is as clear as glass.

10 Cover the frame with a large box to keep dust and insects off. Leave it to dry for twenty-four hours, then you can cut off the dry drips with a sharp blade.

PERFUME BOTTLE AND BOWDER BOWL, TONBRIDGE ANTIQUES, ROSEVILLE, NSW

Florals on Country Furniture

BY SUSANNE BARRETT AND JOANNA HERCUS OF COUNTRY FOLK

The florals on the chest have been painted in soft, warm tones and would suit any piece of old pine furniture. Before painting remove any doors and sand the timber well.

Materials

- suitable piece of furniture
- round brush, size 3
- flat brush, 2.5 cm (1 in)
- white transfer paper
- stylus
- old lint-free rags
- varnish
- Matisse background paints: Antique Green, Antique Blue, White
- Feast Watson Satin Varnish
- steel wool, 0000
- Liberon wax
- Jo Sonja's Artists Colors: Pine Green, Turners Yellow, Warm White, Indian Red Oxide, Napthol Red Light, Raw Sienna, Opal, Moss Green, Sapphire

Method

See the Painting Designs on pages 27–29.

Preparation

1 Lime the sides and trim of the chest with a soft green-blue made from the three background colours mixed as follows: White: Antique Green: Antique Blue in the proportion 2:1:1. Mix the liming colour, then add sufficient water to make a runny cream consistency. Wet the area to be limed with water, using the 2.5 cm (1 in) brush, then wipe the area with the rag to remove any excess water. Now, apply the liming mix quickly with the same brush, then wipe over with the rag to leave a soft hint of colour on the pine. First try this procedure in an inconspicuous area because the time left before wiping back with the rag varies greatly, depending on the weather.

2 Transfer only the main outlines of the pattern to the furniture, using the white transfer paper. Don't press too hard when transferring the pattern or you will leave indentations in the pine. Note that the patterns on the ends of the drawers are reversed.

Painting

Use the round brush for painting the design.

Note: * means you should add just a touch of colour in the following instructions.

For the leaves

The leaves are painted with a mix of Pine Green plus *Raw Sienna, and Moss Green plus *Raw Sienna. The darker leaves are at the centre of the pattern and the lighter ones are towards the edge. Keep the leaves fairly transparent and add the highlights while the base coat is still wet. To highlight the dark leaves, load the brush with the dark leaf colour mix, then pull it through Moss Green. Turn the Moss Green upwards and stroke commas as shown on the design. Keep this subtle. To highlight the light leaves, use the light leaf colour mix plus Warm White and proceed as for the dark leaves. The dark leaves are lightly outlined with Moss Green and the light leaves are outlined with Opal.

For the ribbon

The ribbon is painted with a dark pink colour made up of a 1:1:1 mix of Indian Red Oxide: Napthol Red Light: Raw Sienna. Keep the paint watery and side-load your brush with Warm White. The ribbon should be transparent.

For the roses

1 Complete one rose at a time so that the paint remains wet. Base coat with a light pink, made up of a 1:1:1 mix of Napthol Red Light: Raw Sienna: Opal. Shade the throat and the base of the bowl of the rose with the base coat plus Indian Red Oxide.

2 While the base coat is still wet, emphasise the shape of the rose with comma strokes. Load your brush in the light pink base colour and pull it through Opal. Keep working in the wet paint so that individual strokes are not too obvious. Do not wash your brush during this process.

3 Finally, pull the still-dirty brush through Warm White for highlight strokes. Refer to the design for the stroke work

For the blossoms

Complete one blossom at a time as for the roses. Base coat in a medium yellow, made up of Turners Yellow plus *Raw Sienna. Shade at the centre by patting the brush in the rose shading mix. Highlight with a mix of Turners Yellow plus Opal, pulled through Warm White. The centre dots are Raw Sienna and Turners Yellow.

For the tulips

Base coat with the blossom mix. With the yellow still in your brush, pick up a side-load of red (made up of Napthol Red Light plus Raw Sienna) on the tip of the brush. Outline the tip of the tulip petals with the red, working one petal at a time so that the red paint will not dry before you flatten the brush and pull the red down towards the bottom of the tulip. Dry-brush pale yellow (Turners Yellow plus Opal) up from the base of the tulip.

For the small blue flowers

Each flower is made up of two or three small commas with a dot of Turners Yellow at the centre. The colour is Sapphire plus *Raw Sienna plus Opal to make a soft blue.

Finishing

1 Add transparent filler leaves wherever they are required to fill a gap. These should be both leaf-shaped and simple commas.

2 Varnish all vertical surfaces with two coats of varnish and all horizontal surfaces with three coats. When the varnish is completely dry (allow several days after the final coat), wax with the Liberon. Apply the wax with the steel wool, leave it for twenty minutes, then buff with a soft cloth.

Side Panel Design

Drawer Design

Chest Top Corner Design

Pansy Hat Box

PAINTED BY LILLY PILLY FOLK ART, COFFS HARBOUR

Posies, pansies and hoops all add a touch of Victoriana. Here, they are combined with Regency stripes and even a little touch of crocheted lace for the total effect.

Note: This is mostly a flat-brush project, suitable for the intermediate to advanced folk artist.

Materials

* wooden hat box
* Jo Sonja's Artists Colors: **Warm White, Turners Yellow, Napthol Red Light, Burgundy, Indian Red Oxide, Diox Purple, Paynes Gray, Moss Green, Teal Green, Black**
* flat brushes, sizes 1 cm (³/₈ in) and 1.2 cm (¹/₂ in)
* liner brushes, sizes 0 and 1
* round brush, size 2
* palette
* pencil
* tape measure
* Magic Tape
* transfer paper
* stylus

Method

See the Painting Design on the Pull Out Pattern Sheet.

Note: If no brush is specified, use a brush appropriate to the area you are painting.

Preparation

1. Remove the handles, hinges and clasp fittings from the box and set them aside.

2. Mix a large amount of Warm White and Turners Yellow. Paint the lid and sides of the box with at least three coats of this cream colour. Paint the bottom and the handle with Indian Red Oxide. Allow to dry thoroughly.

3. Measure and mark for the Regency stripes in the following arrangement. Mark ten 5 cm (2 in) wide stripes which will be left cream and ten 4 cm (1¹/₂ in) wide stripes to be painted with Indian Red Oxide. Stick rows of Magic Tape down the sides of the box at these marked lines to give you a clean edge. Paint the wide Regency stripes and the narrow stripes with Indian Red Oxide.

4. Paint the inside of the box in the cream or Indian Red Oxide.

5. Paint the hoop, using the size 1 liner brush and the Indian Red Oxide. The hoop pulls the whole design together so don't make it too narrow.

6. Transfer the painting designs to the box, using the transfer paper and stylus.

For the leaves

Note: It is hard to get a good colour coverage when painting a dark colour over the cream. It is best to go over the leaves a second time when the first coat is dry. See this demonstrated on the worksheet on pages 32–33.

1. Using the 1 cm (³/₈ in) flat brush loaded with half Moss Green and half Teal Green, blend the colours on the palette. Keep a balance between not having enough moisture or having so much that the brush is oozing with paint and you lose control. Using pressure to form the bumpy edge of the leaves, paint from the base to the tip on one half, then turn the brush over and paint from the tip to the base on the other half. Make sure your brush is angled upwards and outwards so your strokes follow the natural direction of the veins. Be consistent with where your light falls (the Moss Green sections).

2. When both coats are dry, add veins, using the size 0 liner brush and a mix of Moss Green and Warm White.

For the pansies

Note: The pansy petals are painted in the order in which they lie in nature: first the two back petals overlapping, then the two side petals overlapping, then the last petal in the front.

1. Many colour combinations are possible, but here there are just six. As you paint a pansy, remember to paint a bud or two in the same colours, scattering them around the lid and the sides. Use the 1.2 cm (¹/₂ in) flat brush.

#⅜" Flat

Put pressure on brush to form humps, keeping centre firm, not like this.

#2 round for flip overs.

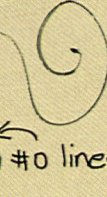

#0 liner for tendrils

This row has only been painted once.

Remember to keep this design below lid line.

Pansy bud #⅜" flat

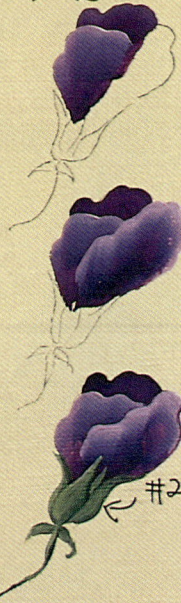

#2 Round

hail spots may be added with Red Earth.

#½" flat.

Brush fully loaded c̄ T.R.O. blended one side W.W., one side Black.

I paint the last
tal from one
de, breaking
f and then
ning from the
ther side

Tidy up some of
the edges with
#0 liner. Flipovers
with a #2 round side-
loaded with white.

I try to keep the lace neat but I like
the "hand-made" look.

Diox P. with Black blended
into Burg. & White.

Paynes Grey, Diox P.
& White.

Gillen 94

Pansy A   Paint the back and the side petals with Turners Yellow. Blend in a little Indian Red Oxide for the deep colour in the centre of the petals. Reverse the brush for the front petal so the deeper colour is at the edge and blend in a little Diox Purple as well.

Pansy B   Load the brush with half Turners Yellow and half Napthol Red Light. Paint in the same way as pansy A, blending in a little Diox Purple on the Red edge.

Pansy C   Mix a little Black into the Diox Purple. Load the brush fully with this mix, then blend one edge into Warm White and the other edge into Black. Paint in the same way as pansy A.

Pansy D   Load the brush fully with Indian Red Oxide, then blend one edge into the Warm White and the other edge into a little Black. Paint in the same way as pansy A.

Pansy E   Load the brush with two-thirds Burgundy and one-third Turners Yellow. Blend, adding some Diox Purple at the Burgundy edge. Paint in the same way as pansy A.

Pansy F   Load the brush with Paynes Gray, blend one edge into Warm White and the other edge into a mix of Diox

Purple and Black. Paint the two back petals with this mix, placing the lighter colour at the centre. For the side and front petals, reverse the brush so the outer edges of the petals are lighter.

2 Add the finishing detail to the pansies and the leaves following the worksheet on pages 32–33.

For the tendrils
It is a good idea to practise this technique on a piece of card first. Moving your arm from the shoulder and using the size 0 liner brush, make some freehand swirls in Teal Green, mixed with a little Moss Green. It is best not to trace these in, but to refer to the pattern for size and general direction, then just let yourself go!

For the crocheted lace
Paint in the crocheted lace around the rim of the lid with Indian Red Oxide, using the size 0 liner brush.

The Lady in Red

PAINTED BY KATH CONNELL

A book on medieval art inspired Kath to paint this beautiful glove box, because the elegance and simplicity of the lady in red had such appeal.

Materials

- ❧ Paul Foster glove box
- ❧ Jo Sonja's Artists Colors: Rich Gold, Pale Gold, Brown Earth, Warm White, Napthol Red Light, Cadmium Scarlet, Paynes Gray, Burnt Umber, Yellow Oxide
- ❧ Jo Sonja's Clear Glaze Medium
- ❧ base paint, Black
- ❧ flat brush, 2.5 cm (1 in)
- ❧ dagger brush, 2 cm (³/₄ in)
- ❧ liner brush
- ❧ flat or round brush, 2.5 cm (1 in)
- ❧ sea sponge
- ❧ varnish
- ❧ beeswax (optional)
- ❧ white tracing paper
- ❧ stylus
- ❧ pencil

Method

See the Painting Design on the Pull Out Pattern Sheet.

Preparation

1 Basecoat the sides of the box in at least two coats of Black, sanding between coats.

2 Paint the bottom and the interior of the box in a mixture of equal parts of Cadmium Scarlet and Napthol Red Light. If you do not want such a richly coloured interior, you could use another colour or you could line the box with fabric.

3 Paint the front and back of the lid with two coats of Rich Gold.

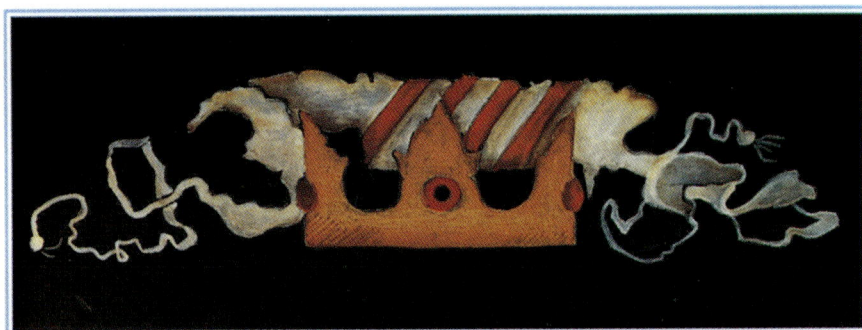

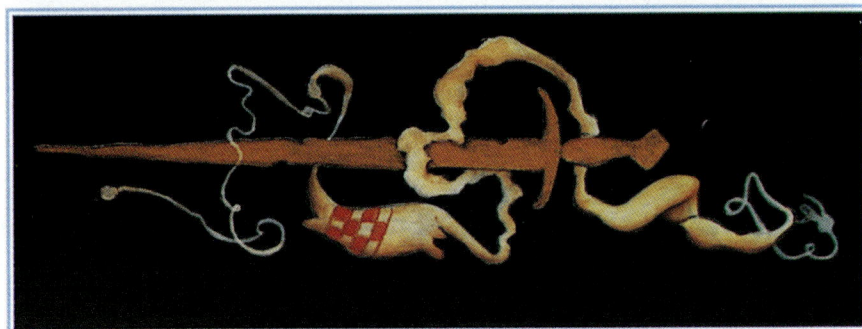

For the design

1 Using the large flat brush, paint the lid of the box with a 3:1 mixture of Brown Earth and Clear Glaze Medium, brushing lengthwise lightly but quickly. Using the damp sponge, pull back some of the colour by sponging very lightly to give an aged look. If this does not work the first time, sponge the lid completely clean and do it again until you have the desired effect. Leave the lid to dry.

2 Transfer the major design lines from the pattern sheet to the lid, using the tracing paper and the stylus. Do not transfer the inner lines of the fabric and the facial features at this time.

3 The gown is a mixture of equal parts of Napthol Red Light and Cadmium Scarlet. Using the flat or round brush, block the gown in, leaving the belt and cloak edging in Rich Gold.

4 The skin is a mixture of Warm White with a touch of Yellow Oxide and a touch of Napthol Red Light. You will not need much, so mix the colours sparingly. Paint on several coats to cover the gold base. When you are painting the fingers, make them long and elegant.

5 Trace the rest of the pattern, the inner lines of the gown and the face and transfer them to the lid of the box, taking care to keep the lines light and precise when you are drawing in the face.

6 Using Paynes Gray, paint in the lines of the gown, making some of the lines heavy and some light, as shown. Using the dagger brush, load the tip and palette blend. Place the tip of the brush on the line and lay down a light shadow. If the gown becomes too dark, load the brush in the Napthol Red Light and put in some highlights on the opposite side to the shadow.

7 Using the dagger brush and Brown Earth with a touch of Napthol Red Light, paint some shadow around the face, under the wimple and the chin. As this is a wash, you will not see the colour on your brush. Add a little more Napthol Red Light and apply it like blusher across the cheeks. The outline is straight Brown Earth, the eyes have a touch of Burnt Umber and the lips are Napthol Red Light. It is important to make the colouring as light as possible. Shade the hands the same colour as the face.

8 Using the dagger brush, highlight the wimple in Pale Gold as shown. This gives the wimple a lovely weightless look that catches the light. Outline the wimple in Brown Earth.

9 The banner with the sword is Warm White, shaded in Brown Earth and Napthol Red Light. The checks are Napthol Red Light. The sword is Rich Gold shaded in Napthol Red Light.

10 The banner with the crown is a wash of Warm White (two coats) to give it a transparent look. It is shaded in Brown Earth and Napthol Red Light. The stripes are Napthol Red Light.

11 The scroll is a series of comma strokes picking up Rich Gold and Pale Gold alternately. The more paint on your brush, the more ornate it becomes. Do not clean the brush between the golds – this gives a lovely range of tones.

12 Finish the box using your favourite varnish. This box has been rubbed with beeswax to give a feeling of warmth and age.

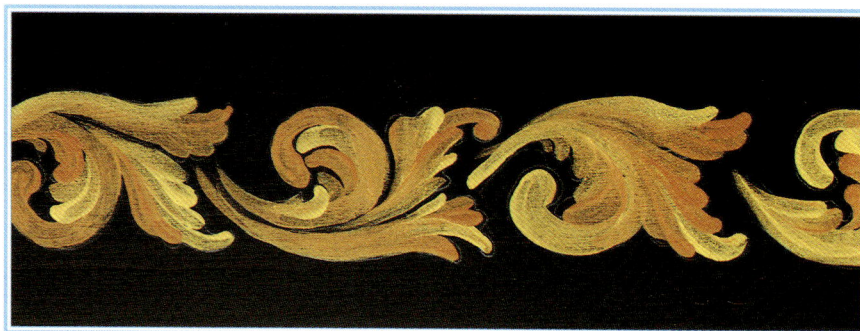

Découpage Spectacle Case

MADE BY GLORIA MCKINNON

Turn a battered old spectacle case or a boring plastic one into an object of beauty that you will be proud to flourish.

We have used Diana Lampe's Embroidered Garden paper, making this an ideal gift for an embroiderer.

Materials

- very plain hard spectacle case
- gesso
- Liquitex Gloss Medium and Varnish
- small rubber roller
- small sharp scissors
- background paper
- suitable pictures
- Clag paste
- Aquadhere PVA glue
- foam brush, 2.5 cm (1 in)
- paintbrush, 2.5 cm (1 in)
- damp cloth
- Wattyl Estapol, satin finish
- fine sandpaper
- steel wool, 0000 grade
- sepia pencil
- car polish or furniture wax (optional)
- lint-free cloth

Method

Preparation

1 Using the foam brush, coat the spectacle case with two coats of gesso. Ensure that the first coat is dry, before adding the second one. Allow the final coat of gesso to dry completely, before proceeding.

2 Using the foam brush again, apply two coats of Liquitex to the spectacle case, allowing each coat to dry before proceeding.

3 Select your pictures. They should be quite small and could follow a single theme. Coat the background paper and all the pictures with one coat of Liquitex.

4 Cut the background paper to fit the spectacle case so that it goes over the lip, but not into the case. For the curved ends, cut darts into the paper, cutting out the excess fullness so the paper will sit smoothly. Take care to cut the darts so the edges meet evenly with little or no overlapping.

Découpage

1 Mix three parts Clag paste to one part Aquadhere until you have a very smooth consistency. Using the foam brush, coat the spectacle case with the glue mixture. Place the background paper on the case and smooth it down. Position the cut ends so they meet neatly. Using the roller, gently work over the case, pushing out any excess glue. Keep wiping the roller to keep it free of glue.

2 Carefully cut out the pictures with the small scissors. Make sure all the edges of the pictures are very neatly cut. If there are any white edges showing, you can colour these with the sepia pencil.

3 Position the pictures on the background paper in a pleasing arrangement before you begin to stick them down. Note that the pictures will come down the sides of the case and over the curved ends. You may need to treat these in the same way as the background paper, cutting small darts to allow them to sit smoothly. Glue the pictures into place, using the roller each time to remove excess glue.

4 When all the pictures are glued down, clean off any excess glue with a damp cloth, then cover the piece with two coats of Liquitex, allowing it to dry completely between coats.

5 Apply twelve to fifteen coats of Estapol, using the paintbrush. Sand vigorously to remove any high points. Continue to add coats of Estapol, sanding again after every two or three coats until you are pleased with the finish.

6 Gently rub over the piece with the steel wool. Add a final coat of Estapol or finish your spectacle case with car polish or furniture wax.

GOLD GLASSES FROM FRIVOLITIES, MOSMAN, NSW. TEACUP FROM MOSMAN ANTIQUE CENTRE, MOSMAN, NSW

Chocolate Box

PAINTED BY LYN FOSTER

This dramatic black box, decorated with lush roses and touches of lace, provides wonderful storage with an elegant touch.

Materials

- 35 cm (14 in) round box
- white transfer paper
- stylus
- background paint, Black
- 5 cm (2 in) sponge brush
- round brushes, size 2 and size 4
- 6 mm (¼ in) dagger brush
- good liner brush
- Jo Sonja's Artists Acrylic Colors: Teal Green, Warm White, Pine Green, Burgundy, Storm Blue, Yellow Oxide, Brown Earth
- palette or old saucer

Method

See the Painting Design on the Pull Out Pattern Sheet.

Preparation

1 Using the sponge brush, base coat the box with two coats of Black, sanding the box lightly between coats. It is very important that you have a smooth surface on which to paint.

2 When the base coat is dry, trace the design from the pattern sheet and transfer the design to the box, using the transfer paper and stylus. Do not transfer the dots and the fine lines of the ribbon or lace.

Painting

1 Base coat the main ribbons and the lace insert with a mixture of Teal Green and Warm White, mixed to a light/medium colour. Make sure you keep the mixture smooth. When the base coat is dry, paint in the crosshatching, using the liner brush and Warm White. Do not paint any of the dots.

2 Base coat the bow with a lighter version of the ribbon base coat. Shade the ribbon with Teal Green. Dry brush in the highlights, using Warm White.

3 Base coat the leaves in a mixture of Teal Green and Pine Green. Using the same colour and the liner brush, paint in the stems.

4 Using the liner brush and a medium mix of Warm White and the leaf base colour, and starting at the tip of the leaf, pull strokes two-thirds of the way down the leaf. Add a little more Warm White to the mixture, then lighten the tips of the leaves with little fine lines.

For the roses

1 Base coat all the roses in a mix of Burgundy, Yellow Oxide and Warm White, varying the amount of Warm White to produce three different shades.

2 Using the dagger brush and a mixture of Burgundy and Yellow Oxide, float in the centre of the flowers.

3 Load the size 4 round brush with the base colour, side-loaded in Warm White. Pull in the back petals of the rose first, around the shaded centre, then paint the front and outer petals. When the petals are dry, dry brush in the highlight in Warm White.

4 Reinforce the centre of the roses using the dagger brush and Brown Earth.

5 Load the liner brush with Brown Earth and tip in Yellow Oxide, then pat in the stamen to the rose centre. Add highlights with a few dots of Warm White.

For the daisies

Paint the daisies in Warm White with a Yellow Oxide and Burgundy centre. Paint the directional dot in Warm White.

For the fillers

Paint the fillers in Storm Blue with a Warm White centre. Paint the directional dot in Storm Blue.

Finishing

Paint in the dots on the lace and ribbons, using the stylus.

Découpage Box

MADE BY NERIDA SINGLETON

This box is a beautiful example of découpage – the creative composition of paper cutouts on a surface which is then covered by numerous applications of clear varnish, allowing the image to glow through.

When découpaging a box, always keep the focus of the design on the top and front of the box with less emphasis on the bottom and sides. The background can be painted, covered with wrapping paper or constructed from pictures.

Materials

- box (with the fittings removed)
- curved cuticle or surgical scissors, finely pointed
- 10 cm/4 in rubber roller
- 2.5 cm/1 in imitation sable brush for varnish
- Liquitex Gloss Medium and Varnish OR Atelier OR Matisse MM7 OR Jo Sonja Gloss Medium Varnish for Découpage for sealing
- Clag School Paste and PVA adhesive
- Goddard's Cabinet Makers Polish
- Wattyl Danish Wax (optional)
- sponge applicator or cheap brush for sealer and gesso
- gesso
- glass paper
- wet and dry sandpapers, 280, 600, 1200 and 2000 aluminium oxide
- clear varnish (various brands of varnish and polyurethanes will do)
- tack cloth
- steel wool, 0000
- Blu-Tack or Faber Castell's Tackit
- oil-based colouring pencils: sepia, black
- sponge and towel
- protective mask and goggles
- mineral turpentine and brush cleaner
- beeswax stick or wood putty
- Scotchbrite scourer
- brass fittings
- sheets of no. 10 white cardboard
- 3M microfine or micromesh finishing kits
- artists acrylic paints (if you are painting a background), and sea sponge
- black fineline permanent marker pen OR gold fineline permanent marker pen
- workable fixative (optional)
- waxed paper
- plastic zip folders
- rubber or cork block
- scalpel or paring knife
- muslin cloth
- craft glue
- spray adhesive
- spatula
- wadding
- fabric for the lining
- cutting compound
- electric drill and 2 mm/$^1/_{16}$ in drill bit
- ribbon

Method

Preparation

1 Mark the top and bottom of the inside of one side of the box so that it will fit flush when hinged. Check for crevices which may need to be filled with the beeswax stick or wood putty. Apply the filler with the spatula. If you are using putty, be generous with it because it will shrink as it dries. Beeswax is preferable for filling as it does not shrink.

2 Sand the box well with glass paper, then sand it lightly with no. 280 wet and dry sandpaper and wipe it clean.

3 If you wish, you can apply the gesso before lightly sealing the box or you can paint the background with at least two coats of artists acrylic paints, applying each coat in a different direction. If you are not applying gesso or painting the background, eliminate step 3.

4 Seal the box with your choice of sealer, drawing the sealer out well so that no bumps and lumps are evident. Seal the inside and rims of the box as well.

5 Seal the images sparingly on both sides of the paper before cutting them out. Seal the back of the picture first. Allow it to dry for ten to fifteen minutes, then sparingly seal the front of the picture.

6 Cut out each picture precisely, eliminating the inside areas you don't need before cutting the outline. Cut with the curve of the scissors pointing away from the picture. Remove all the white background at the edges of the image.

7 Make a cardboard template for each surface of the box. Using the Blu-Tack, experiment with the design, beginning with the focal picture and building up the complementary images until you are satisfied with the effect.

Note: Pictures which cover a corner and travel down the sides will have to be mitred at the corners. Make sure you have enough pictures before you begin gluing.

Gluing

1 Using a 3:1 mixture of Clag paste and PVA apply a generous amount to the box surface and smear it with your fingertips until it is silky. Before placing the pictures down, make sure that you have not missed any areas and that there are no hard lumps of glue. Place the first picture, then massage with a little extra glue on top of the picture until the glue becomes tacky and the bonding between the picture and surface takes place. Distribute the glue evenly behind each picture.

2 Add a little more glue, then using the rubber roller, roll with very gentle pressure from the centre of the picture out to the edges. Don't use too much pressure when you are rolling as this will eliminate all the glue and you will have no adhesion. Hold the surface up to the light to check if there is any accumulated glue or air behind the picture. Keep the roller clean by wiping off built-up glue.

3 Using a damp sponge, wipe any excess glue from the surface of the picture. The glue will appear dull when held in the light. Do not glue over a wet picture.

4 Repeat steps 1 to 4 until all the pictures have been glued down. Check that there are no dull patches.

5 Allow the box to dry, then check each picture for white edges. Colour any that you find with an appropriately coloured oil-based pencil and smudge the edge if the line is too definite. This will allow all the images to blend together.

6 Sign and date your work with the marker pen. If you are using a gold fineline pen, spray your signature sparingly with workable fixative when the ink is dry, otherwise it will smear under the sealer. Allow the fixative to dry.

7 Seal all the surfaces sparingly. If you are not able to finish gluing and have to leave the project overnight, clear away all the glue, pencil any edges, then seal the object. This will prevent the pictures from losing adhesion, especially at the corners, and also alleviates the possibility of damage. (Vermin are instantly attracted to the excess glue on the pictures.)

8 If you do not use all the sealed pictures, place them between sheets of waxed paper and file them into plastic zip folders. The sealer will stick them together if you don't use the waxed papers to separate them.

Varnishing

1 Use the protective mask and have good ventilation in the area in which you are working, when you are varnishing. Using the fine brush, beginning applying the varnish at the top, using light sweeps in one direction. Do not stir the varnish or polyurethane unless so advised in the manufacturer's instructions. Satin, matte and water-based products should be thoroughly stirred to incorporate the sediment. Gloss is a harder and more suitable product.

2 Be sure to brush out any accumulation of varnish where the top and sides of the box join or at the rims. Check for drips. Wipe the excess varnish from the brush on to the side of the varnish tin. Using the tip of the brush, lightly sweep across all the surfaces to remove any air bubbles and excess varnish. Be sure to work in a good light. Support both sections of the box raised on tins to allow the air to circulate around them while they dry.

3 Allow twenty-four hours drying time between each coat of varnish. Before applying the next coat of varnish, wipe the surface dust particles off with the tack cloth. Alternate the direction of each coat of varnish.

4 When you have applied twenty coats, begin sanding with the no. 600 wet and dry sandpaper. Sand lightly in one direction with the wet sandpaper wrapped around a rubber or a cork block. Wipe off the white residue with the damp sponge then allow the box to dry. Colour any white edges, then seal the surfaces and begin varnishing again.

5 Repeat the process of sanding with the no. 600 wet and dry sandpaper and varnishing until the surface is quite flat. This may take somewhere between thirty and fifty coats of varnish.

6 Change to no. 1200 sandpaper for the final polishing after the last three coats of varnish have been applied. Remove the excess build-up of varnish at the rims of the box using a scalpel or paring knife. Be sure the surface is uniformly dull – that there are no crevices between superimposed pictures which show tendrils of gloss. If there is still gloss evident, rub with a dry Scotchbrite, then with the steel wool. A cutting compound is also helpful at this stage.

7 For a gloss finish, apply a light coat of varnish, using seven parts varnish to three parts mineral turpentine. Be sure there are no air bubbles in the surface and place the object in a dust-free environment to dry. Repeat this process until the surface is perfectly smooth.

8 For a waxed finish, put a teaspoon each of clear beeswax and the Goddard's polish in an oven to warm them, or in a microwave oven for about twenty seconds on HIGH. Apply the polish sparingly with the dampened muslin cloth and work on only small sections at a time. Dip the cloth in boiling water and buff each section before you move on to the next one. Repeat if necessary. Apply a final light coat of the polish over the entire surface and repeat this often during the curing time to enhance the finish even further. It can take from six to twelve months for an object to harden completely.

Finishing

1 Using the electric drill and 2 mm/ $^{1}/_{16}$ in bit, secure the brass corners. Avoid fittings which are secured with nails – those with screws are the most suitable. Use the drill bit for all the fittings, starting with the corners. Work on the handle and then the top. You will find it easier to manipulate the fittings before the hinges are attached.

To attach the hinges, measure an equal distance from the ends and drill the opposite sides in sequence. Add the clasp – choose one that has a padlock. It is best to secure the top of the clasp and then line up the underneath section to ensure it is not too loose. An antique padlock and handles can add a great deal of style to a box.

2 If you have not taken the pictures over the rim, paint the inside of the box rims with artists acrylic paints. Leave to dry, then apply two coats of sealer, allowing time for the paint to dry between each coat.

Lining

1 Cut ten cardboard shapes for templates, remembering to allow for the thickness of the fabric at each side. Cut 6 mm/ $^{1}/_{4}$ in of wadding the same size as the top and bottom templates. Lightly spray the cardboard with the spray adhesive and stick the wadding to the cardboard.

2 Cut the fabric 1.5 cm/ $^{3}/_{4}$ in wider than the template all around. Mitre the corners by cutting a triangle from each corner of the fabric to allow it to fit flush at the corners when glued. Glue the edges of the fabric to the back of the cardboard with craft glue. Apply the craft glue to the bottom of the box, spreading it evenly with a spatula. Place the fabric-covered template on to the glue and weight it down to ensure adhesion.

3 Now that the thickness of the cardboard, wadding and fabric is determined in the top and bottom of the box, reduce the width of the cardboard templates accordingly for all the sides. The length of the sides will also need to accommodate two thicknesses of extra fabric so keep readjusting them. Do not pad the sides as this will reduce the interior space of the box. Attach the fabric-covered side pieces in the same way as for the top and bottom, but omitting the wadding. Work on each side separately. Secure the sides with craft glue keeping pressure on them until they are firmly stuck. Glue a length of ribbon behind the covered cardboard on one end to hold the box lid open. It is a good idea to do these two ends last.

4 If your box is round or oval with the lip of the lid fitting over the base, make a pencil line around the base of the lip on to the bottom and only paste the pictures to this line. Successive coats of varnish will build up and prevent the lid from fitting properly. The bare areas can be painted in a colour to match the background colour of the pictures or in a colour which coordinates with the lining.

Nerida Singleton has written three découpage books:

- ♣ *Découpage,* Boolarong Publications, Brisbane 1990
- ♣ *Découpage, An Illustrated Guide,* Sally Milner Publishing, 1991
- ♣ *Découpage Designs,* Sally Milner Publishing, 1992, and a calendar
- ♣ *Découpage Calendar,* Five Mile Press & Sally Milner Publishing, 1993

Lace Fan

PAINTED BY ELIZABETH WHITE

Delicate painted lace makes this lovely heirloom fan.

Materials

- ✿ practice board, 25 cm x 35 cm (10 in x 14 in)
- ✿ base paint in the colour of your choice (pictured is Forest Green)
- ✿ Jo Sonja's Artists Colors: Warm White, Pearl White
- ✿ round sable brush, size 8403
- ✿ liner brush
- ✿ palette or an old saucer to use for a palette
- ✿ white transfer paper
- ✿ tracing paper
- ✿ stylus
- ✿ water-based varnish
- ✿ tiny tassel

Method

See the Painting Design on the Pull Out Pattern Sheet and the Painting Guide on page 48.

Preparation

Base coat the board with two coats of background paint, sanding between coats. Using the transfer paper and stylus, carefully transfer the basic outline of the design, centring it on the board. Press lightly and do not trace on the flower design at this stage.

Painting

1 Tip the round brush into the water, then work it into the Warm White. Carefully paint in the basic outline of the design.

2 Reload the brush by flattening it into the watery Warm White and side-load with a heavier Warm White. Softly and lightly paint the top sticks (shown as a broken line on the pattern).

3 Transfer the rest of the flowers.

4 Using Warm White, completely wash in the long guards on either side and the short sticks. Using Pearl White, completely wash the two long side guards again.

5 Using Pearl White, wash half of the short sticks (left side).

For the lace

1 Using Warm White and the liner brush, follow step 5 in the painting guide to complete the crosshatching and line work in the lace. Leave all the dots and the comma work until last.

2 Load the brush with watery Warm White and paint a very thin ribbon under the roses.

For the rose

Load the brush as for the ribbon and follow the stages in step 7. The crosshatching is lightly painted on after the leaves are completed.

For the leaves

Work with the brush flat and loaded with watery Warm White, keeping the leaves very small. Paint as shown in step 8 of the painting guide.

For the forget-me-nots

Load the brush with thick Warm White and paint, following the stages in step 9 of the painting guide. When all the roses, leaves and forget-me-nots are completely dry, lightly wash over this area with watery Warm White. Work the forget-me-nots on the sticks and the right guard.

Finishing

1 Using the stylus, place the dots on the lace scallops.

2 Paint all the commas last.

3 Allow all the paint to dry thoroughly before varnishing the whole design.

4 Drill a very small hole in the handle at the base of the sticks to attach the tassel.

Step ① Outline Step ②

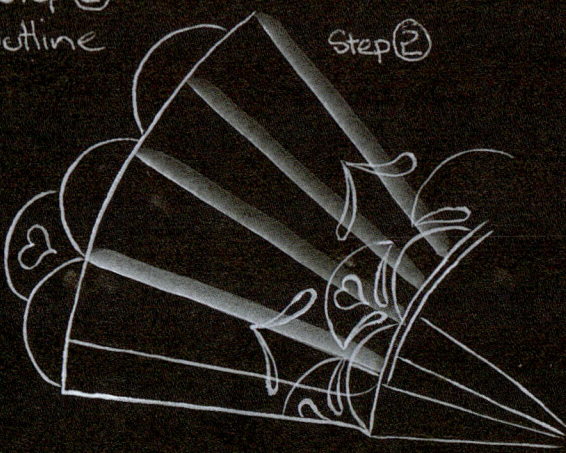

SIDE GUARDS

STEP ③
Warm white wash

STEP ③
Pearl white wash

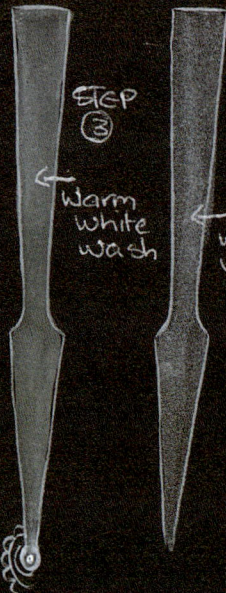

STICKS

STEP ⑧
Warm white wash

STEP ④
Pearl white ½ wash

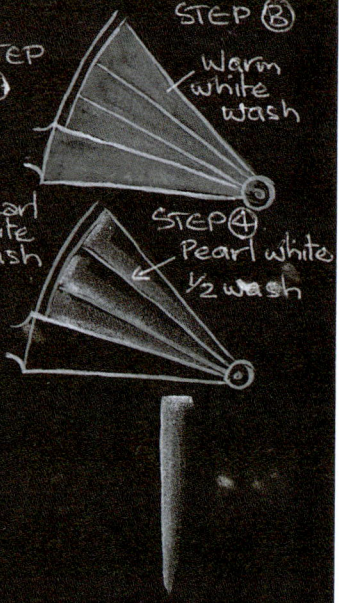

LACE :- Step ⑤

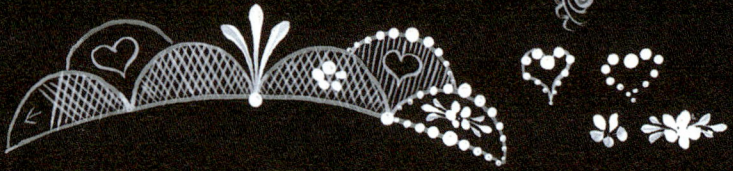

RIBBON - Step 6

ROSE :- Step ⑦

LEAVES. Step ⑧

FORGET-ME-NOTS:- Step ⑨

LOWER LACE

FORGET-ME-NOTS ON LOWER STICKS:- Step ⑩

COMPLETED SECTION OF ROSE AND FORGET-ME-NOTS